An American's Guide to European Travel

Jonathan A. Jones

An American's Guide to European Travel

Jonathan A. Jones

This book is dedicated to my parents, Charles and Jeneen Jones who instilled the love of travel in my siblings and me.

An American's Guide to European Travel
2022 Edition
©2022 Jonathan Jones, All Rights Reserved
Printed and bound in the United States of American

All rights reserved. No part of this publication may be reproduced, stored in any retrieval system, or transmitted in any form or by any means, mechanical, photocopying, recording, or otherwise, without permission in written form from the publisher, except by a reviewer, who may quote brief passages in a review to be printed in a magazine, website or newspaper.

For information contact Floating Spark Publishing
1660 N Hunter Dr
Olathe, KS 66061
www.JonathanJonesAuthor.com

admin@JonathanJonesAuthor.com

Available in these formats:
ISBN: 978-1-7364633-6-9 (Paperback)
ISBN: 978-1-7364633-7-6 (Kindle)
ISBN: 978-1-7364633-8-3 (E-Book)

Library of Congress Control Number: 2022912054

Although the author and publisher have made every effort to ensure the accuracy and completeness of the information contained in this book, we assume no responsibility for errors, inaccuracies, and omissions, or any inconsistency herein. Any slights of people, places, or organizations are unintentional.

Acknowledgements

Jill Jones
Jennifer Healy, Editor
Polly Blair, Editor

Advanced Readers
Matt Brown
Lexi Jones
Mike Zaring

Contents

What does this book cover?...9
The Basics..13
Booking Your Travel...17
Safety...23
Language...27
Money and Spending...29
Lodging..35
Eating...39
Tipping..43
Transportation...47
    Traveling by low-fare airlines..................................... 47
    Traveling by Train 49
    Renting a Car 51
    Driving on the Wrong Side of the Road 54
    Using the subway systems 55
    Using the bus systems 56
    Taxis and Ride Sharing 58
Don't be the Ugly American...61
Conclusion...63
Appendix...65
Bibliography...69
About the Author...71

What does this book cover?

The idea for this book came to me while on a trip to Greece. My wife, Jill, and I were discussing the many challenges, tips and tricks we had learned on our many European vacations. We came up with several things that anyone who didn't travel frequently would need to know before they embarked on European travel. This got me thinking about all those issues and how I could communicate them through a short publication that could be easily carried along as someone travels through Europe. I believe that I have distilled these issues down to the most commonly "googled" questions of people getting ready to travel in Europe.

What are my qualifications to write this book? I'm not a travel writer, nor do I have my own TV show or podcast. I'm just an "Ordinary Joe" who has traveled throughout Europe frequently. This book will not include hotel or restaurant recommendations that often pay for inclusion in other travel books or blogs. I'm not famous and nobody is paying any special attention to me when I travel. The story I tell is the story of an ordinary person navigating the challenge of traveling abroad.

My father was a professional travel agent, and he and my mother traveled frequently, sometimes taking the whole family, sometimes traveling without us. They instilled the love of travel in myself and in my siblings. I made my first trip to Europe while in high school. That trip would be followed by nine more trips to the continent over my adult years. Two of my three children studied for a semester in Europe, one in the Netherlands and one in England. We also hosted a foreign exchange student from Spain whom we have visited in her home country after her time in America. Lastly, my sister married a man in the U.S. Army, and they were stationed in Germany for a few years. Of course, when all these people were living overseas, we had to go and visit them. I love history, which is abundant in Europe, and have thoroughly enjoyed all of these trips.

Just to be clear, this book covers Europe. England and the rest of the United Kingdom are considered part of Europe. The United Kingdom (England, Scotland, Wales and Northern Ireland) presents some interesting issues for travelers since they left the European Union in 2020. I could do an entire book on traveling in the United Kingdom, but for this effort I'm only going to break England into separate chapters when necessary.

Figure 1: European Union, as of May 2022. The list of countries in and out of the European Union (EU) is not static. There are several countries currently applying for membership and others like the UK in 2020 who have or are considering leaving the EU.

England is not the only country in Europe who is not in the European Union (EU). The following countries make up the European continent: Albania, Andorra, Armenia, Azerbaijan, Belarus, Bosnia and Herzegovina, Georgia, Iceland, Kosovo, Liechtenstein, Moldova, Monaco, Montenegro, North Macedonia, Norway, Russia, San Marino, Serbia, Switzerland, Turkey, Ukraine, Vatican City. Not all of these are in the EU. The importance to the reader as to countries who are in the

EU, versus not in the EU, is that the countries in the EU use the same currency, the Euro (€). The fact that a country is not in the EU is not a big deal for the reader and most of the advice given in this book will still apply. The big difference is that these countries do not use the euro, which means that for each non-EU country you will need to consider the exchange rates for the local currency rather than the euro. More on this topic later.

Another issue with a country not being in the EU is that it is likely their border and customs procedures will differ from EU countries that share borders. I'm not going to go deep into border procedures for each country, as they are constantly changing, largely in response to geopolitical events. Expect to have your passport checked when crossing a country's border, while some borders within the EU might be truly open, most will at least want to check your passport. Expect more stringent rules if you are passing from an EU country to a non-EU country. While traveling in Europe, you should always have your current passport with you. If you don't have one, you need to get one. Take care of this early, as it can take six to ten weeks to apply for and receive a new or renewed passport. Details for obtaining a passport can be found at https://travel.state.gov/content/travel/en/passports/how-apply.html.

Without further ado, let's get started. Hopefully this book will take some of the stress out of travel and help you make the most of your upcoming trip to Europe!

The Basics

Get your passport and make sure it is not expired. As mentioned in the previous section, you will need a passport. Get one today if you plan to go to Europe. You will not be able to go without one. You should also check to see if there are any travel requirements that you must meet in order to travel between the U.S. and Europe at the time you start planning your trip. In 2022, due to the Corona Virus pandemic, travelers entering Europe were required to be fully vaccinated and be able to produce vaccination cards to prove that status. Also, in 2022, the U.S. Government required travelers coming into the U.S. to be able to show a negative Covid test within 24 hours of entering the country. There are many covid testing sites in Europe, but make sure you plan this out as you will not be allowed on the plane to come home if you cannot produce this negative test. The test should only be about $10, and you should be able to get your results back almost immediately. Each country will be a little different. Don't leave this to chance, I recommend confirming with someone, such as the hotel, in the country where you will be the night before you are scheduled to return to the U.S., where you will be able to get this test, how long the results take, and how much it will cost. **Travel requirements are continually changing, check with your airline for updates. For example, as of June 2022, the Covid test requirements have been lifted. I would not be the least bit surprised if it is put back in place when the next serious health issue arises.

Get to know the metric system. All of Europe, and most of the world, uses this system of weights and measurements. Of course, in the U.S. we do not. In the back of this book, I have included several charts which give you a conversion table for key measurements that you might find useful while in a "metric" country. I did not try to recap the entire metric system, but key things like temperature, distance, weight and volume are in the back of the book. An example of one measurement that gave us trouble while in Europe was the temperature. You will not see Fahrenheit anywhere; the temperature is always shown in Celsius. We like to watch the news or look at printed forecasts to help us decide what to wear for the day. The problem became, we had no idea how Celsius converted to Fahrenheit. The chart below, which is also in the back of the book, gives you an idea of how temperatures in Fahrenheit convert to Celsius.

Celsius to Fahrenheit	
Celsius	Fahrenheit
40	104
30	86
20	68
10	50
0	32
-10	14
-20	-4
-30	-22

 Dress for your Destination. Many travel books will tell you that in certain countries you should not wear shorts or short-sleeves or some other normal item of American clothing. I have never seen this to be a problem. With the international nature of society today, no matter where you go, you will see people dressed in all sorts of ways. I recommend trying to dress neatly and conservatively, but shorts are typically fine. If it would be strange in America, it would also be strange in Europe. For example, we don't wear swimming suits to the grocery store in America and you shouldn't in Europe either. It is best if you try to hide the fact that you are a tourist. Wearing sports team shirts or even tourist shirts bought on your vacation can make it clear to a thief targeting tourists that you are not local. Looking like a tourist is not a sin, but from a safety perspective, the more you can avoid it, the better off you will be. More about safety in a later chapter.

 If you follow these simple guidelines, you will not have any issues. The one exception to that rule is if you intend to visit churches or other religious locations, some of these may have dress codes which may include rules such as no shorts, hats etc.

An American's Guide to European Travel

Packing. Obviously, what you pack is going to depend on where you are going. You are going to pack very differently for Sweden than you would for Greece. In this section I'm talking more about how much you pack rather than what you pack. A traveler should consider how they plan to get around Europe and then determine how much to pack. If you are traveling at a higher expense point and you plan on taking taxis directly to the door of your hotel, large suitcases are okay. However, if you are trying to travel more cost efficiently, you may want to rethink that large suitcase. Large suitcases are very difficult to navigate down crowded streets, onto buses and through subway stations. If you feel like you will be doing a significant amount of walking to and from your hotel, consider smaller suitcases that are easier to carry and maneuver. Consider pairing this smaller suitcase with a backpack that can hold some items as well.

You will also need to consider the size of your suitcase when you rent a car. More about renting cars later. Many of the "economy cars" that are available to rent in Europe will simply not hold more than one large suitcase. These cars are very small.

You will need an electrical adapter. All European countries use a different type of electrical outlet that we use in the U.S. They use a two-pronged plug, while in the U.S. we use a two- or three-pronged plug. The European, type C, plug delivers 220 – 240 volts of electricity. The U.S. type A and B plugs deliver 100 – 127 volts. You will need to purchase an adaptor to use any of your electrical devices in Europe.

Figure 2: On the left you see a U.S. Type B plug. On the right, is a Type C plug used in Europe. It is very rare to find any Type B plugs in Europe. You will need an adaptor.

You will find a wide variety of choices when you look for an adaptor. I would recommend going "middle of the road" in terms of cost. You don't need the "top of the line" adaptor, but don't buy the cheapest one you can find either. We have had more than a few electrical devices ruined when used in Europe with a cheap adaptor. We have been lucky that the main casualties for us seem to have been hair dryers, which were relatively inexpensive. You don't want to go cheap and lose a laptop or some other expensive device. Some hotels may have USB plugs, but don't count on them. I recommend getting an adaptor that has multiple type B plugs as well as a few USB plugs. You shouldn't have to spend more than $15 - $25 for a good adaptor.

Figure 3: Example of an adaptor with multiple type B plugs and USB plugs.

<u>Always carry some change.</u> We will talk more about this later in regard to tipping, but you should always carry a small amount of change in Europe. The reason for this is that you find many places where public restrooms cost a few coins to use. Public bathrooms in European countries run the gamut of what you might expect. I have seen some public restrooms where you basically just go behind a wall and do your business. These "restrooms" were for both men and women. Bottom line, carry some change. You don't want to be caught having to go to the restroom without any change.

Booking Your Travel

How you decide to book your travel is up to you and more importantly your budget. There are generally four options as to how you might choose to book your trip.

1. Book it all yourself using mainly internet resources
2. Book through an American travel agency
3. Book through a travel agency in the country you are visiting
4. Travel with a tour group

Certainly, booking the travel yourself allows you to have the most control over your itinerary and the costs that you will pay each step of the way. The obvious downside is that if something goes wrong, there is nobody to contact if you need assistance. I have booked travel through options 1-3 and will talk extensively about those. I have not traveled as part of a tour group. I will touch briefly on that option but have no personal experience with that option. In my younger days I booked everything myself because I felt I was able to have more control over the costs. In my later years I feel it is worth the extra money to pay a professional to set everything up. I have also learned over time that the difference in cost is often not that great, and the reduced stress is well worth a few extra dollars.

If your trip is simple, for example you are flying into one city and staying there for a week, do it yourself. It is when the trip gets complicated that you might consider using a travel agency. In my experience, going through a travel agency takes a significant amount of the stress out of a complicated itinerary. When you book a trip yourself, all of the details are left up to you, if an agency does it, it is on them to make sure that they have covered everything.

On our last trip to Greece, there were several moving parts.
1. Travel to Athens
2. Athens Hotel
3. Four-day cruise

4. Two nights in Santorini
5. Flight back to Athens
6. Two nights in Athens Hotel
7. Flight back to U.S.

    In planning this trip, I went back and forth with my European travel agent to set the itinerary. They asked how long we were planning on being in Greece, what we wanted to do, and how much we wanted to spend. With this information, they recommended an itinerary. My wife and I discussed their suggestions and made some tweaks to the plan. The travel agent then took our changes and adjusted the itinerary. In addition, we told them what type of hotel we were comfortable staying in (how many stars), and that is what they booked for us. All of these tweaks led to price changes which we had the opportunity to accept or reject or do more tweaking to get the price where we wanted it to be. The bottom line when considering the use of a travel agent is that you are still in control, you are just calling on their expertise to help you get the best trip possible for your money.

    A complicated itinerary, such as ours in Greece requires the coordination of several moving parts. As part of our trip, we required transportation to several different places.

1. From Athens airport to Athens Hotel (about an hour)
2. From Athens hotel to Athens Port (about an hour)
3. From Santorini Port to Hotel (1/2 hour)
4. From Santorini Hotel to Santorini airport (15 minutes)
5. From Athens Airport to Athens Hotel (about an hour)
6. From Athens Hotel to Athens Airport (about an hour)

    The point of this story is that if you book yourself, you need to remember and have a plan for all these transfers. Your trip does not work without them, and you may not have a great idea of exactly what you need or how to set these up. Can it be done? Of course it can, but be prepared to spend a considerable amount of time talking to local taxi lines, bus companies, train lines etc. All of these local companies will claim that they can get you where you want to go, just remember that you will also be carrying luggage. Your luggage may be a problem if you are going up and down subway tunnels or getting on and off multiple buses.

Buses may be full or may not be running on time. Will it be a problem if you are a little late? Do you need to plan to be there hours before your flight, cruise, or train departure just to make sure that nothing prevents you from getting on that vehicle? If you are booking these transfers yourself, hotel clerks can be a valuable resource. They should be able to tell you the best way to get somewhere. Do not leave this until the last minute. Figure out your transportation plan for that leg of your journey as soon as you arrive in a city. Your cruise/flight/train will leave without you if you are not there.

On our Greece trip, our travel agency set everything up for us. So, in my mind, using a travel agent gives you all the benefits of a group tour, without having to deal with all the people. Some of whom could annoy you to no end before the trip is over. A month before our trip, we received a packet with all of the details of our trip. Those details included the fact that we would be met at the airport by someone holding a placard with our name on it and that person would take us to our hotel in Greece. At 8 am the next morning, a driver would be in our hotel lobby waiting to take us to the cruise ship port. We knew at every stop how we were getting from one place to another and who was going to get us there. Zero stress!

You have two choices for travel agencies, either an American agency or a European agency. The service that they provide is basically the same. Each will also tack on a fee to your travel for their services. With an American agency you can be a little more confident that you have chosen a reputable agency that will meet your needs. In Europe there is a bit more of a risk in that you don't know which agencies are good and up to the task of planning your trip. Do your best to vet a European agency. Check reviews and anything else you can find about an agency before booking with them. The benefit of having an in-country agency is there is literally someone right there that you can call, that can usually solve any issues you may have immediately. In our case there were usually two people meeting us at each stop, one "tour guide" and one driver. This was important to us because as we arrived at the Santorini airport there was a large crowd of students, basically blocking access to the counter that we needed to get to. We did not know if they were in line or not. Our tour guide pushed right through the crowd and took us to the gate. We would have likely stood behind this group for quite a while before eventually figuring out that we needed to go through them to get to our counter.

Of course, the difference between the two options is money. With a travel agency American or European, you set the amount you want to spend, and they do the best they can with the budget you have given them. It will generally cost you between 5% and 10% extra to use a travel agent. Some agencies will charge a flat fee while others will charge a percentage of the total cost. In my opinion, well worth it, as almost all of the stress goes away. That said, I understand that some are traveling on a budget. I also understand some people like the challenge of getting around in a foreign country. My father was a travel agent and loved trying to figure everything out on the fly. I enjoyed this challenge more as a young man, but less as an older adult.

I didn't touch too much on the option of using an American travel agency because I think they will do basically what the in-country agency will do but they do not have the local knowledge of the best hotels, the right transportation modes etc. Basically, they are charging a similar fee to that of the European company for simply doing the internet searches that you could have done. One other thing to remember about European agencies is that they will give you a number to call in case you need something. Did you miss your driver? Did he/she not show up? What do you do? You have a number to call. The U.S. agency will probably also provide a number, but it may be 3 am in the U.S. Are they going to answer?

I highly recommend the "in-country" agency route if it is something you can afford. If you are really watching your pennies, you can always compare prices. Map out your trip on your own and then get a price from your travel partner. Don't forget to include transfer costs, and estimate high, as it will always cost more than you think to get where you need to go in a timely manner.

Regardless of how you book your trip, you are generally responsible for your own airfare. Most anyone who has traveled in the past 15 years knows how to book travel on the internet. Booking for a European trip is no different. I will point out one item regarding flights to keep in mind and that is the timing of your arrival. We always try to set our flights so that we are arriving in our destination country in the morning or early afternoon. Do your best to not arrive very late at night or very early in the morning. At those times of day, there is nothing to do and nowhere to go. You can't check into a hotel, you can't go to attractions, and you will be left just sitting in the airport waiting for the sun to come up.

Arriving in the midafternoon is the best. That way you can go to your hotel, drop your bags and go out and take a walk after sitting on a plane for several hours. You will be jet lagged. Depending on where you are traveling, the time will be anywhere from 6 – 9 hours ahead of U.S. time. The local time may be 1 pm, but to your body clock, the time will be something like 4 am. You also will likely not have slept well on the flight. You will be tired. Allow yourself a short 1-hour nap in the afternoon, but no more. You want to get your body clock adjusted as soon as possible so you can enjoy your vacation. After your nap, you should be able to enjoy the evening and then make it an early night. Don't be surprised if you wake up at 3 or 4 am the next morning. Do your best to go back to sleep in an effort to correct your body clock.

Regardless of how you choose to plan your trip, you also need to think about the best time to go. I recommend going to Europe in what is called the "shoulder season". Traveling in shoulder season means that you will be traveling either at the beginning or the end of the peak European travel season. Thirty two percent of all tourist dollars in Europe are spent in July and August. The shoulder season, for most European countries, is late May through mid-June, and late September through early October.

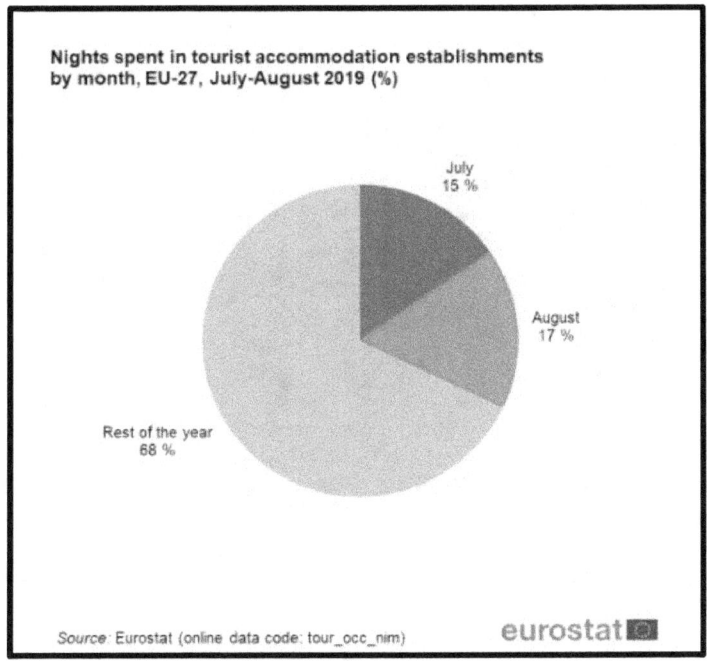

Figure 4: Nights spent in European Hotels by Month

This time frame is when the tourist season is either just starting up or winding down and generally means prices may be lower, crowds will be smaller, and lines will be shorter. It is during this shoulder season that tourist destinations are still trying to attract visitors, which may make it easier to find deals and bargains on all sorts of travel expenses. The downside might be that the weather might not be perfect for certain locations. The tourist season happens at a certain time for a reason. Sometimes that reason is based around the weather. For example, beach type locations are most popular during the hot summer months. If you are willing to go when it is not quite "beach weather" you may be able to get some discounts.

Safety

In today's world, there is nowhere on the planet that we can guarantee our absolute safety. Terrorist attacks are being plotted in every country almost every day. Each individual country does the best it can to thwart those attacks and to make sure citizens and visitors are safe when traveling inside their borders.

If you are looking for someone to say that traveling to a certain country is 100% safe, you will never find that. To be fair, you would never get that in the U.S either. If you were reading a European book about visiting the United States, that book might tell you not to visit Chicago due to the danger in that city. As a former Chicago resident, I find that comical as I never felt threatened during my time in Chicago. That said, I also knew that there were certain areas of Chicago that were much more dangerous than others. My solution, I didn't go to those dangerous areas.

Europe is no different. Most large cities will contain areas that it would be best to avoid. More importantly, just use the same common sense that you would use in any city in the U.S. Be smart and use common sense in your actions wherever you might be. Don't keep all your money and credit cards in the same wallet/purse/etc.

The U.S. State Department web site, www.travel.state.gov lists all the countries in the world and a travel rating that it has set for American travelers in that country. The site uses a four-tier system. The levels of which are:

1. Exercise Normal Caution
2. Exercise Increased Caution
3. Reconsider Travel
4. Do Not Travel

As of May 2022, most countries are labeled as Level 1. Some examples of Level 2 countries would be France and Germany who have recently had terrorist related events. Many Central American countries, such as Honduras and Guatemala are ranked as level three, and as you would expect, several countries in the middle east such as Iran and Iraq are listed as level 4. This is a good website to check out before you travel, but don't get scared away just because a country is listed as a level 2. The United States would probably be at least a level 2 if our state department was forced to rank the U.S. Our country might also be a level three given the rash of violent crimes and mass shootings that have occurred in the Covid and post-Covid time frames.

While violent crime in most level 1 and 2 rated countries is rare, street crime is much more common. Pickpockets are everywhere in Europe just like they are in the U.S. If you are in a large crowd, be mindful of your wallets, purses, backpacks etc. I speak from experience having had my pocket picked on a subway car in Rome during a trip to Italy.

In my case, we were getting onto a very crowded subway train. I bent down to pick up my daughter and a man bumped into me as the train started moving. I didn't feel a thing, but as soon as I got off the train and felt my back pocket, I knew he had gotten my wallet. In this instance, I had ignored my wife's advice to wear an around-the-neck wallet. You can bet I still hear about that from time to time. The bottom line is to be mindful of your possessions in crowds. I'm a grumpy old man and still like my wallet in my back pocket, but now when I'm in a crowd, I at least move my wallet to my front pocket and keep my hand in that pocket. I know it's still not as good as a money belt or a more secure necklace wallet, but it makes it more difficult for a thief.

No matter what precautions you may take, you still might be a victim of a street crime like pickpocketing. To make sure your vacation is not ruined by this occurrence, make sure that you have multiple credit cards that are not stored in the same place. If you are traveling as a couple, each of you should carry a copy of each card. This helps because if you need to cancel that card, you will have the physical card with the number to call. You should also keep the contact numbers of your credit cards in your phone or somewhere in your luggage so you can call immediately if your card gets stolen. In my case I did not do any of these things and the thief had already charged $1,200 worth of merchandise on my card before I could find a phone and call the credit card company.

Of course, you will usually not be responsible for these fraudulent charges as long you call the credit card company as quickly as possible.

An American's Guide to European Travel

This is another reason to take a credit and not a debit card. With a debit card, that $1,200 would have come right out of my checking. Yes, I would have eventually gotten it back, but not until the bank's claim process had finished.

Some general safety tips for travel in Europe or anywhere in the world

1. Be aware of your surroundings.
2. Don't walk down dark streets late at night.
3. Dress like a local as much as possible.
4. Never show large amounts of money in stores or restaurants. In fact, avoid carrying large amounts of money.
5. Keep your money hidden. Wear a money belt or necklace wallet as opposed to a fanny pack. Fanny packs make it very clear to a thief where your money is.
6. Instead of a handbag, carry a cross body shoulder strap purse.

Language

As Americans, we are fortunate when we travel to Europe and throughout the rest of the world because there are often at least some locals who speak our language. English is the language of business and thus is often a language that is taught in schools as a second language. This means that even in the most non-English speaking countries in Europe, there are many people who at least speak a little English. Many, but not all, European countries have road and street signs, both in their native language and in English.

This does not mean that you should just expect everyone to speak enough English to help you do whatever you are trying to do. The farther off the beaten track you are going in your travels, the more likely you are to encounter situations where you will have to resort to using hand signals and pointing at things to communicate. Be ready for this.

Before you travel, spend some time learning some basic words in the language of your destination. You don't need to be fluent but learn some basics. Know how to say "hello" and "goodbye", "thank you" and "you're welcome". You should know how to ask common questions, such as "Where is the bathroom", or "How much is this?". Just knowing a few common phrases will make things easier for you when you come across a situation where you can't find anyone who speaks English. How would you make a non-English speaker understand, "Where is the bathroom", without being able to use words? Think about that for a minute.

Modern technology has also given us another way to get over language barriers by creating apps that will translate something to another language by simply speaking the words into your smartphone. Make sure you check out options to download certain phrases on the app just in case you don't have cell service when you need it.

Money and Spending

Most European countries use the euro (€) as their form of currency. The United Kingdom made things a little more difficult when in 2019 they decided to exit the European Union and go back to using British pounds. This complicates things a little if traveling to the UK and then into other European countries. There are also a small handful of other European countries that continue to use their own form of currency rather than the euro. If in doubt, check online to make sure what your destination uses for its currency.

Figure 5: Euro Currency. The black and white picture doesn't do it justice. The bills are all different colors and sizes. They also have one-and two-euro coins.

First, you should know the exchange rate. I'm going to use the euro for my examples in this chapter, but you can easily use the exchange rate for the British pound or other currencies if you are headed to places that still use their own currency. When this book was published the exchange rate for U.S. dollars to euros was $1 = €1.1 euro. Which was as good, from an American standpoint, as it has been for quite some time. This means that if something costs €10, it costs $11. The euro is easy to deal with since it usually tracks closely with the U.S. dollar. In the not too distant past, the exchange rate was more like €1.3 to $1. In those days, the math changed, but the process didn't. At that exchange rate, if something cost €10, it actually cost an American traveler $13. The exchange rate can dramatically affect the cost of traveling in Europe for an American. You should be able to quickly translate a country's currency into dollars, so that you are aware of what you are spending. I try to keep a chart in my head, or on paper, of certain dollar amounts, for example:

€1	= $1.1
€10	= $11
€50	= $55
€100	= $110

As of May 2022, a near one-to-one exchange rate means that the euro to dollars conversion chart is not as important. However, over time that rate will change and the more it changes, the more the chart becomes valuable. You will need to make your own chart if the rate changes when you are ready to begin your travels. You will also need to create your own chart if you are visiting a country that does not use the euro. For example, the chart for the Icelandic Krona, in May of 2022, would look like this:

kr100	= $ 0.75
kr1000	= $ 7.58
kr5000	= $ 37.92
kr10,000	= $ 75.85
kr50,000	=$379.25

As you can see, with the Icelandic currency, all the numbers will not be quite so easy to figure out in your head. Currency exchange rates move every day, not dramatically, but be aware that they are regularly changing. The chart below shows the history of the euro to dollar exchange rate for the past 10 years.

10-year History of Euro to Dollar Conversion Rates

Date	1€ =
December 31, 2013	$1.33
December 31, 2014	$1.33
December 31, 2015	$1.11
December 31, 2016	$1.11
December 31, 2017	$1.13
December 31, 2018	$1.18
December 31, 2019	$1.12
December 31, 2020	$1.14
December 31, 2021	$1.18
May 17, 2022	$1.10
Average	$13,173

I recommend getting some euros before leaving home. This way you are prepared when you arrive in your destination country. Most banks will sell you currency if you request it at least a few weeks in advance. You don't need to get enough cash to cover your entire trip but get enough to cover the first several days. This allows you to be ready with tip money and any other situations that may arise in which cash is needed. You can get more cash from local ATMs later in your trip when it is needed. Keep your initial batch of euros spread out in different safe locations. When we travel, we split the euros into four piles. My wife carries one, I carry one, one goes in my suitcase and the last pile into my wife's suitcase. This way no matter what happens, lost bags, lost purse or wallet, or if something is stolen, we still have cash available for our use.

When you change money with your bank before leaving, there will be a fee for that service. There are often money changing booths at most airports that you could use for this service, but they will likely charge a higher fee for their services than you would pay at the bank. If you need money and can't find an ATM, many hotels are also willing to change money, but be aware the exchange rate often benefits the hotel.

For most of your purchases in Europe, use a credit card, not a debit card. Debit cards, if they work at all, will be treated as a credit card in

Europe. I have had issues with a non-chip debit card in things such as toll booths and other automated type transactions. For this reason, my advice is to leave your debit card at home. Using a credit card gives you arm's length security from your bank account, just in case some thief knows how to get the pin. I like to take two credit cards, with my wife and I each carrying copies of each card. If one is lost or stolen, we always have another one. If you travel alone, don't keep the two credit cards in the same bag or purse. Keep them separate, one in your purse and one in your suitcase. This way if a bag or purse is lost or stolen, you can easily access the card you had stored in the other one.

Credit cards are common in Europe and most modern stores and even market vendors will take them. Mastercard and Visa will work everywhere, a few establishments will take American Express. Very few vendors, if any, will take Discover. Most of the restaurants and shops in Europe use the "tap" method of processing your card. It is best if your card has the chip and tap functionality. Most cards in the U.S. today have a chip, but I've seen some that do not. If yours doesn't have the chip, get one that does before you leave for Europe. The tap method is a benefit for travelers because the card never leaves your hand. No more wondering if a dishonest employee wrote down your card number while they had the card in the back room.

When you use a credit card in Europe, the bank is basically taking the transaction in euros, converting it to dollars and then charging your card the total amount. On your statement or online banking app, you will see the final charge in dollars rather than the cost in euros. Your credit card bank then will apply an international transaction fee on top of the purchase price. You will be able to see these on your online account or on your statement later. The international transaction fee is usually somewhere near 3%. Not a big deal on small purchases but it will start to add up when you pay for larger items like train tickets, hotel bills and rental car charges. Three percent of $10 is only thirty cents, but three percent of $1,000 is $30. You can avoid this fee by applying for and receiving a credit card that waives all international transaction fees. There are many free cards with this feature, and it can be a big money saver if the card you use in Europe waives these fees.

Use credit for most things over €10. For anything below that amount, use cash as this will be quicker and keep the vendor from having to pay the vendor credit card fee for such a small item. Cash should also be used for tipping. There are many people you may want to tip on your travels. The practice of tipping will be covered in more detail in a later chapter. I like how the euro is different from the dollar in that they have €1, and €2 coins. These coins are great for tipping. The lowest denomination of paper money is €5, followed by €10, €20, €50, and €100. I'm told that there is also a €500 bill, but I've never seen one.

When you start to run low on cash, simply go to an ATM and get some more. The ATMs in Europe are easy to use and almost all of them have a button to push which allows you to process your transaction in English. Make sure you have established a pin for your credit card prior to leaving for Europe. Most cards allow you to do this online, but some send the code in the mail, so it needs to be done a few weeks before your departure. Remember, that no matter how you change money in Europe, you are likely paying a fee for that service. That is why credit cards, with no foreign transaction fees are the best way to conduct your business in Europe. Using a no fee credit card means that you are only paying the cost of the item plus the current conversion rate of the currency for your purchase.

Even if your card has no transaction fee and you use an ATM in Europe, you will still likely be charged an ATM fee by the local bank. There is no way around this. The ATM fee is likely to be around $10. For this reason, limit the number of times you use the ATM. Don't get €20 out of the machine because after the $10 ATM charge, you have basically paid a 50% surcharge for that $20. Plan ahead and get larger amounts when you use the ATM. When I travel, my goal is to have enough cash when I leave home for several days. When I'm running low, I will visit the ATM one time and get enough to cover the remainder of the trip.

Try to use up all of your euros before leaving Europe. When your vacation is nearing its end, figure out what you still need cash for, i.e., driver tips, bellman tips, bus fares, etc., and hold that amount out. With that amount off to the side, use your remaining cash to pay for meals, souvenirs, and other expenses. I recommend using up your euros because changing the euros back to dollars when you get back to the U.S. means that you will be paying another fee to change it back. So, in effect, you will have paid a fee to change it into euros and then another fee to change it back into dollars. You will lose money on both sides of that transaction. If you have small amounts like €15 or €20 left, simply keep it in a plastic bag in the cupboard and save it for use on your next European adventure.

Lodging

Finding lodging in Europe is a bit more difficult than it might be finding it in the U.S. Do not expect the same size of rooms nor the amenities that we are used to here in the states. Hotels in Europe are generally more expensive and finding lodging for more than 2 or 3 persons can be tricky. Pay attention to the bathrooms in the hotel you are booking, particularly with older hotels. As Americans we find it hard to believe that many hotels in Europe may come with a shared bathroom and shower facility. Watch carefully, especially at the lower end of the star ratings, to make sure that the room you are booking has a private bath. It is quite common in these lower-end, older hotels to have only one shared bathroom on each floor. If that is a deal breaker for you, you may have to find a different hotel.

While every country and indeed, every city may be a bit different, many of the hotels in Europe do not generally have rooms that accommodate four or more persons. Particularly in the cities, it is not uncommon for hotels to consist of rooms designed for 2 or 3 persons. Finding lodging for four or more can be a challenge. European hotels usually have one double bed, or maybe even two twin beds. The U.S. norm of two queen beds will be difficult to find in Europe. That is not to say that they do not exist. There are hotel chains in Europe that may have more U.S. style rooms, but they are not the norm, and they are generally considerably more expensive than other hotels. The European rooms are smaller because most of the buildings are older and the rooms in the past were just smaller. The hotels are simply making the best of the limited amount of space that they have available.

A typical European hotel may also be missing a few of the amenities that we are used to in American hotels. Oftentimes, the bed and a couple nightstands will be the only furniture in the room. Again, this is because the room itself is very small. Following that trend, the bathrooms will also likely be quite small, resembling the bathroom on a cruise ship or a mobile home. In today's world, pretty much all hotels have wi-fi. Of course, like in America, the strength of the signal varies widely. If you find a hotel with a decent wi-fi signal in your room, you will likely be using it regularly to buy online tickets, check out transportation schedules, or just look up facts about the area you are visiting. If you are at a hotel with a weak wi-fi signal, I would recommend finding a spot, either in the hotel or somewhere else nearby where you can easily access the internet to perform simple tasks that come up during your stay.

European hotels will usually include a television, but don't be surprised if it is a smaller, older model as opposed to the large screens that are now standard in U.S. hotels. The channels will vary. If you are in a non-English speaking country, feel fortunate if you can receive one or two English speaking channels. In some of these countries you may only get a few channels and it is very possible that none of them will be English speaking channels.

There are other amenities that we often expect in our U.S. hotels that may or may not be present in European hotels. Hair dryers may or may not be in each room. The hotel booking should make it clear that there is a hair dryer in your room. If it is not listed, don't expect it to be there. If a hair dryer is a must for you while traveling, contact the hotel and confirm that their rooms do not come with one. If not, be prepared to bring your own. (don't forget about a power adapter as discussed earlier in the "Basics" chapter.)

Like in the states, some hotels will be clean and kept up very nice, while others will not. The star system for hotels of one to five stars is used in Europe just as it is in the U.S. Don't be surprised if a 4-star hotel in Europe does not meet your expectation of a 4-star hotel in the U.S. In my opinion, the star system does not necessarily match up when comparing ratings between the two countries. In my mind a 3.5 star in the U.S., would actually be a 4.0 star in Europe. The cost of room usually follows the stars just like it does in America.

I mentioned earlier that finding rooms for larger groups can be difficult and expensive. Some European hotels will have no rooms for these groups while others may have large rooms, but there may only be one or two of these rooms in the entire hotel, and they fill up fast. If you are traveling with a group of four or more, there are a couple points to keep in mind. If you really want the hotel experience, book early. This allows you to have the pick of the hotels with larger rooms before they are booked solid. Don't be surprised that the cost for these rooms will be higher than the cost for the rooms for fewer people. Another option is to book multiple rooms. As you can imagine, this gets even more expensive. The rooms in many European hotels are expensive anyway and booking two of them doubles your cost.

Another recent option is to book through a vacation sharing site like www.airbnb.com or www.vrbo.com. Particularly for families or groups of 5 or more, this is an excellent way to save money and often can be a better fit for your family or group. I have traveled with family groups of more than five on multiple occasions and we have had great luck using these sites. These units often come with kitchens as well which can be another way to save a little money when feeding the entire group.

Budget conscious travelers might consider a hostel. Hostels are like boarding houses and are available in almost all European cities. A hostel gives you a place to sleep and access to a generally shared bathroom for a very low cost in comparison to a regular hotel. The reason the hostel is so much cheaper is that you will not be in a private room or have a private bath. You will likely share a room with several other travelers. You will have your own bed, but it will be in a room with several other beds that will be occupied by other travelers, of all genders. The bathroom is usually down the hall and will be shared by all persons staying on that floor. While there are certainly stories about bad things happening in hostels, they are generally safe and well run and can be a great option for someone traveling on a budget that enjoys meeting and interacting with new people. Make sure and check online reviews for a hostel to ensure that it appears to be safe and well-run.

Wherever you stay in Europe, there will be some lodgings that you like and others that do not live up to your expectations. I can only suggest you read prior reviews thoroughly, be leery of places where there seem to be issues with owners or staff, and make sure you know key facts such as how far it is to the nearest train or bus station. Also note how far the location is from the sites you are visiting in the city. The closer the better. You don't want to spend half of your time on vacation simply getting from one place to another.

Eating

Let me be honest with everyone who is reading this book. I am a meat and potatoes guy; I like American food and I don't particularly like the food in other countries. One of the things I really look forward to at the end of an international trip is going home and getting some good old American food. I know there are many out there who will blast me for not talking about Italian food or French cuisine, but I am who I am. That said, as a traveler, I know we must eat. This section will discuss some of the tips and strategies that you might use to make the most of your money and time while exploring the food of where you may be.

Most hotels in Europe will provide breakfast. These "hotel" breakfasts" will usually consist of a variety of pastries, cheeses and lunch meat. While some will include hot items, most will not. Don't expect pancakes or omelets or other typical American breakfast items. Large American breakfasts are not something that will be easy to find in Europe. The standard European breakfast is similar to the standard hotel breakfast that I have just described.

First of all, sitting down for a meal is a big deal for many European countries. If you walk the streets and squares of cities like Paris, Athens, Rome and Barcelona you will see hundreds of small cafés with their tables out front on the sidewalk with all chairs facing the street. The Europeans love to watch the people walking on the street and the position of the chairs gives them this view. The locals will be there most of the day, not just eating but sometimes just having a tea, coffee or beer.

Europeans eat late. Normal dinner times start at around 7:30 pm and end between 9:30 or 11 pm. Most Americans don't like to eat that late, which works out well for American travelers because it is often easier to get a table, particularly at night, if you want to eat from 5:30 - 7:00 as opposed to later when all the locals are going out to eat.

Most European eateries in walking districts will have menus displayed for anyone to look at before deciding to eat at that establishment. Many will also have salesmen out front trying to get people into the restaurant. Their pitch will be similar to the old carnival barkers. "Step right up folks, see the bearded lady,". These "salesmen" will tell you about their menu, how great their food is, and anything else that they can come up with to try and entice you into their establishment. Don't be pressured by these folks. Have a price point in mind then pick a few items that you can look at in a menu to see how their prices stack up with other competitors.

For example, in Italy, look for spaghetti with meatballs and find the price for that dish. Since that dish is a staple in Italy it should be on just about every menu.   Once you find that dish, you can compare restaurants to see the true cost of eating there. If the spaghetti with meatballs is higher at Café 1 as compared to the price at Café 2, you can probably assume that the overall cost of Café 1 is higher than that of Café 2. As mentioned, many of the large cities will have hundreds of these cafés all right together on the same street, so don't try and look through every menu. Pick a few places that you want to look at and compare prices and ambience and pick one. Some will be good, some will not. That's how life works.

If you are a soda junky like me, you have a rude awakening waiting for you in Europe. Coca Cola is a very popular brand in Europe and is available pretty much everywhere. Other brands such as Pepsi and Dr Pepper are not as easy to find, not impossible, but not as easy. Pepsi is usually in stores, but rarely available in restaurants. My favorite drink, Mountain Dew, is nowhere to be found in Europe. Other flavors like orange are generally available but be aware that the orange flavor in Europe will not taste like what we are used to in the U.S. Bottom line, like everything else, be ready for soda to taste a little bit differently.

Another difference with cost implications is that in Europe, they don't generally have soda fountains. So, if you are used to your "mega big gulp" every morning you are going to be disappointed. Outside of places like McDonalds, I have never seen a regular restaurant with a soda fountain. If you order a Coke, you will usually get a single can or bottle. The size of these cans or bottles is also smaller than we are used to. In Europe, the standard serving size for a soda is 330 ML. This equals 11 oz in America. Our standard can in the U.S. is 12 oz. For those of us soda junkies, that single ounce seems like a lot. For me, when dining in Europe, the soda is usually gone before I even get my food. I generally drink water with my meal because I don't want to pay for another soda.

Also be aware that when you order one soda, you get one soda. There are no "free refills" in Europe. If you want another Coke, you will pay for another coke at €3 – €5 or whatever the price was for the first one. Water is sometimes included and sometimes not. If they pour you a glass it is likely included. If they bring a bottle, expect to pay for that bottle and any others they bring after that. Also don't expect ice with your drink. Sometimes you will get a cup with ice. Sometimes you won't. Even when you do get ice, it will likely only be a cube or two. If you want more ice, ask for "extra ice" up front.

Eating at a typical sit-down restaurant in major European cities can be expensive. We found that in a city like Paris, sitting down in one of the sidewalk cafés was almost cost prohibitive for our family on a regular basis. There are other strategies that you can employ to reduce the food costs on your trip.

1. If you have kitchen facilities in your lodging, you may be able to get some staples and eat a meal or two a day there. The cost of food in grocery stores is a little higher but taking this route could significantly reduce the food costs on your trip. It's also kind of fun to go to a local grocery store to see the difference in the product offerings and the stores themselves.
2. For breakfast, walk to a local bakery and get fresh rolls or pastries. You can either take these back to your lodgings or eat them on the sidewalk with a fresh cup of coffee.
3. For lunch or dinner, make sure to try sidewalk lunch counters. These "order at the window" places often have the same food as the expensive restaurants but at far less expensive prices since they don't have to employ waiters or pay rent on large eating areas. This method also gives you a way to try certain things without spending $20-$30 to do so. In our travels, we often eat at this type of place for lunch and then at a regular restaurant for dinner.
4. While each country is different, fast food could be an option. Some countries, like Germany and the United Kingdom have many fast-food places. Others like France and Greece don't have nearly as many. If you desire fast food to be one of your main dining options, check the maps to see if there are fast food restaurants near your lodgings.

I will leave the recommendations of the food in various countries to those that enjoy food experiences more than I do. That said, realize that each country has its own cuisine. If you are near the ocean, you will see menus filled with seafood. It's no different than in America. Be as adventurous as you desire. Food will generally be more expensive in Europe than what you are used to in the US. Don't forget to include food in your budget for your trip, particularly if you are traveling with a larger group.

Tipping

Now that we have discussed eating in restaurants, let's move onto the next question that usually gets asked. What about tipping? Do I tip in Europe? How much do I tip? Who do I tip? My guess is that these questions are some of the most searched for on the internet by travelers preparing for a trip to Europe.

First, make sure you check and make sure that "service" is not already included on the bill. I have not seen many restaurants that include this in the bill, but some do. If "service" is included, no tip is necessary. Don't be surprised in Europe to see the owner working in the restaurant most of the time. While Europe does have "chain" restaurants, they are rarer than here in the U.S., where a very large percentage of all restaurants are franchises of a chain.

I wish I could give you a clear and defined answer on what to tip. The truth is that the answers are going to vary by situation, by country and by your personal tipping philosophy. Ask almost anyone in the travel industry and they will tell you that you must absolutely tip. In my opinion, this is workers sticking up for each other. The reality is that in European countries you will often find people who, by their actions make it clear that they do not expect a tip. Tips in Europe are not expected each and every time like they are in America. In the U.S. our reason for tipping is that our wait staff workers rely heavily on their tips since they make far less in hourly wages than other workers. In effect, the restaurant is not paying them much at all, but they get to keep their tips, which makes up for the low hourly wage. This is not the case in Europe. While every country could be a little different, for the most part, the wait staff in European countries are paid a regular wage. This difference also causes differences in service. For example, in the U.S. your waiter is usually responsible for most aspects of your eating experience. He/she is working for your tip. In Europe, you may eat at an establishment where one person takes the order while another delivers the food, while others may fill up your water and bring the check. You may not see the person that took your order again.

Basically, they work as a team to serve the customer. Quite frankly, it's a better system.

So, is the answer "don't tip"? I don't think so. My personal tipping philosophy in the U.S. is that I tip wait staff 20%. I very rarely penalize a server for having a bad night or bad food. I've had bad days at work and made some mistakes as well. How would I feel if my employer decided to take 10% of my pay away? The server counts on that money to pay their bills, feed their kids etc. That said, your philosophy on tipping is your own. I'm telling you about my general philosophy so you can see how I adjusted that philosophy when traveling in Europe.

My philosophy in Europe is tip all waiters 10%. Ten percent in Europe is an excellent tip. There is nothing wrong with tipping a little less. Service personnel in Europe will be a bit more appreciative of any tip, simply because it is not the norm in their country. Do not leave the tip on the credit card. In fact, you will rarely, if ever, get asked if you want to add a tip. Restaurants will run your card for the exact amount of your bill, hand you a receipt then wish you well and walk away. This is why you carry coins and small bills. As a comparison to my philosophy, Rick Steves, the famous travel writer, recommends tipping 5 – 10% on his travel site. (Steves,1)

Leave the tip on the table, this way you can be assured that the server or the group of servers will actually receive it. My last statement is not meant to imply that restaurant owners are cheating their staff. The reality is that since they don't usually put tips on credit cards, they likely don't have a system which divides the tips up between that server or bartender or whomever else you are actually trying to tip. If there is a specific person in the establishment that you want to make sure gets part of your tip, give it to them directly. I rarely do this and just make sure I leave 10% on the table. If they want to divide it with co-workers that is up to them. The €1 and €2 coins make this easy as a €40 meal means that you are only tipping €4. Oftentimes you will find that you have a pocketful of change, and this is good way to lighten the load in your pocket.

Who else do you tip? This is a very personal decision as it is in the U.S. I recommend tipping the same people you would tip in the U.S., taxi drivers, bell-hops, tour guides, barbers, masseuses, and anyone else that you would normally tip. Most of these people are likely not expecting substantial tips, but a little something is a nice bonus for them. In Europe, it feels like a tip is truly more appreciated than it is in the US, precisely because it is not always expected. I think 10% is a pretty good rule and can easily be applied to all other tipping situations. I will repeat that I feel tipping is a personal decision and you can make your own decision on who and how much you should tip.

Transportation

This topic is a tough one to cover in one small chapter. There are many modes of transportation that you can use and many factors to consider when you plan your transportation. For this reason, I have broken this chapter down into sub-chapters covering a variety of topics. I'm not going to cover bicycles in this section, but if you are a fit person, bikes are a good option for in-city travel. Almost all cities in Europe have places where you can rent bikes. A significant portion of the population uses bikes as their main form of transportation, so drivers are aware of bikes and used to sharing the road with them.

Traveling by low-fare airlines

Europe has perfected the low-cost airline model. In the U.S. we have low-cost airlines that want to act like their European counterparts, but unfortunately their prices are not that much better than the regular airlines. In Europe, you can get very low air fares through these budget airlines. I mean really cheap, as in under $30 to go from London to Rome. The low fare airlines in Europe are a great way to get around the continent if you understand what you are getting into.

These airlines should be used for inter-European travel, don't expect to come back to the U.S. via these budget carriers. They don't go there. However, these airlines will take you just about anywhere you want to go in Europe. The business model is that they will get you where you want to go with no frills. Don't expect a drink, pretzels, an overhead bin to put a bag in or anything else that you might expect is included with a full-service airline.

Luggage is expensive on these carriers and something you should think about before choosing one of these for your travel. The only "luggage" you can take for free on most of these flights is a small backpack (10 Kg or 22 pounds) that can fit under the seat in front of you. If you have more than that, for example a bag that you want to put in the overhead bin, or God forbid, you want to check luggage, you will pay substantial fees. If you do need to take luggage, you need to total all the costs to ensure you are still saving money by traveling with the low-fare airline.

Another thing to be aware of is that these airlines will often not go to the city center of where you want to go. Their routes often take them to old air bases or smaller airports that are a little bit away from the larger airports, sometimes an hour or so out of town. This could mean that getting to your destination may cause you to incur another expense for a taxi or other transportation to get to the city you are trying to visit. Every airline and destination will be different, so when booking, pay attention to exactly where the flight is taking you and make transfer plans accordingly.

There are several airlines in Europe that consider themselves low-fare airlines. Some of the most well-known include:

RyanAir	www.Ryanair.com
Norwegian	www.Norwegian.com
Vueling	www.Vueling.com
Wizzair	www.Wizzir.com
Eurowings	www.Eurowings.com
EasyJet	www.EasyJet.com

The challenge with using these airlines for an American traveler is that we are generally going to have luggage. The luggage makes these carriers a less cost-efficient model than they might be for a student or a backpacker. One scenario where these might be a great choice is for those travelers who have a home base in a certain country. For example, a person who has rented an Airbnb for a week could take advantage of that situation and go for a quick overnight to a different European city. Leave the luggage in the Airbnb, pack a small bag and off you go. Just make sure you know the details of your trip before making the purchase.

Traveling by Train

In this section I'm going to cover traveling across Europe using the train system. There will be a separate section for the subways even though, technically, they are trains also.

Every country in Europe has a train system, the entire continent is also connected via the Eurail system, which is also connected to some of the in-country systems. The map below should give you an idea of the tremendous coverage provided by the Eurail system.

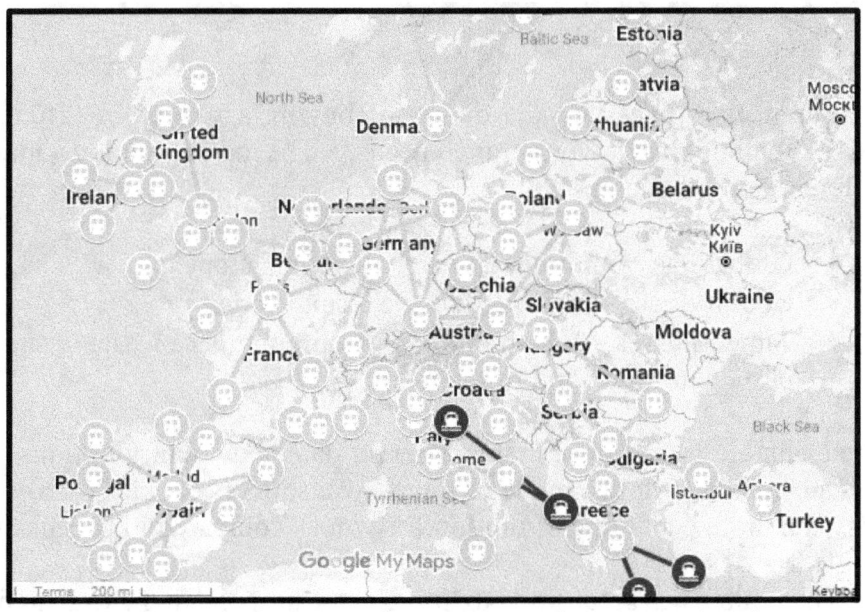

Figure 6: Eurail map, 2022 (Image courtesy of www.Eurorail.com)

The Eurail system is a fast, efficient, and easy way to travel across Europe. Making reservations and planning travel can be done easily through www.eurail.com . The following screenshot shows a sample of the costs and times for some of the most popular routes across Europe.

Train routes	Travel time (by high-speed train)	Reservation	Reservation cost (1st / 2nd class)
Paris to Amsterdam	3hr 20 min	Mandatory	€30 / €30
Paris to Barcelona	6hr 15 min	Mandatory	€48 / €34
Madrid to Barcelona	2hr 45 min	Mandatory	€23,50 / €10
Paris to Geneva	3hr 05min	Mandatory	From €57 / €27
Paris to Rome	11hr 15min	Mandatory	TGV: €45 / €31 Frecce: €10 / €10

Figure 7: Sample of popular routes, times, and costs for Eurail routes in 2022. www.eurail.com

Eurail also gives you the option of buying a variety of different passes that might fit your travel needs. The passes include many different options such as:

- Global Pass – unlimited to anywhere in Europe
- Country Pass – unlimited inside a single country
- Timed Passes – which allow a certain number of trips inside a particular time window

The available passes have many different date and country options. If you are considering this mode of travel, you should consider whether a pass is a more economical solution for you as compared to purchasing single trip tickets.

The train is a great way to travel in Europe. In fact, I highly recommend it as opposed to renting a car, but don't forget to add in the cost for getting from the train station to your final destination. The trains will usually take you to the main station in a large city, but if your hotel is on the other side of the city, you still must get there. We will discuss some local options in the next few pages but don't forget that you will likely be hauling luggage with you at this point in your travels. For this reason, some of the other options might be hard to manage.

As mentioned previously, all European countries have their own rail systems, which may or may not be linked with the Eurail system. These systems are designed primarily for in-country travel. They, like Eurail, also have passes that might suit your needs if you plan on extensive travel inside a given country. All of these in-country systems will have their own websites; you just need to go to their sites to get information for their prices and schedules.

Renting a Car

Renting a car in any country will give you the most flexibility of any of the modes of transportation that you may choose in your travels. But it is also the most expensive and the mode that brings with it the most risk and uncertainty.

The process of renting a car in Europe is very similar to the same process in the U.S. You can reserve your car online through sites like www.expedia.com or www.travelocity.com or at the rental company websites just like you would in the U.S. I recommend at least looking at one of the aggregator sites above so you will be able to see the companies that offer rentals in the location to which you are traveling. These sites will also show you the price differences between the name companies like Hertz and Budget and the small ones that might be available at that location. The smaller companies may be cheaper but be sure and check reviews carefully before booking with an unknown agency. Don't be shocked if a rental agency charges your credit card for a very large deposit, as much as $2000 when you pick up your rental. This is common and is not negotiable with some agencies. If you are a risk averse traveler, renting from an international, well-known agency is a better way to go.

You will be offered insurance for your rental car. You should think carefully about taking this insurance. As a general rule, driving in Europe is more difficult than driving in the U.S. This is true not only because most of us are comfortable with American road signs and traffic procedures, but also because many of our cities were built and designed with automobile traffic in mind. In Europe, the cities can be thousands of years old. The extremely narrow lanes are not developed in any sort of a logical manner as they likely began as horse paths to get from one place to another in the days before automobiles.

Your current auto insurance policy may cover rental cars, or it may not. Call your insurance company and find out if your policy covers rentals outside of the U.S. I recommend talking with someone with your insurer and have them confirm what your policy covers. The language in policy documents can be confusing. If your policy does not cover rental cars in foreign countries, you should absolutely purchase the insurance that is offered from the rental car agency. This will add a significant cost to the rental charge but is something that anyone without insurance should definitely purchase. The risk is just too great, and it is worth the cost.

The reason the risk is high in Europe is due to the differences in the roads as compared to roads in the U.S. The road quality and width vary widely depending on where you are traveling. In large, older cities, expect small, narrow streets, where it seems that only one car can fit. The bad news is they expect two cars to use those streets. The chances of scraping, or denting a car in Europe are much, much higher than in the U.S, where most of our roads are built for SUVs and other large vehicles. Outside of the major cities the roads are more like what we are used to, but you will encounter many single lane roads that present interesting situations such as who is supposed to back up if you meet another car.

If you are traveling across Europe and plan on renting in one country and returning in another, prepare to pay much higher costs for that rental. It is for this reason that I recommend taking a hard look at your itinerary and only renting a car when it is truly needed. This could mean that you only rent a car for a couple days in one country, return that car and then rent another one for a couple more days in a different country. If you can use other modes of transportation and avoid renting cars, I would recommend it. That said, I understand that there are times when it will make more sense to rent a car.

Planes, trains and buses are much more cost-effective ways to travel through Europe. There are several things that make renting a car an expensive option while in Europe. When renting a car, not only will you pay the rental fees, but expect to pay parking fees, tolls and do not underestimate the cost of gasoline. Don't expect large parking lots at hotels, attractions or restaurants in Europe. Finding a place to park on the small roads and alleys is always a challenge.

Gasoline in Europe is very expensive. It is sold in liters, and for comparison's sake, 3.75 liters equals one gallon. In May of 2022, due to the Covid pandemic, the war in Ukraine and other world conditions, the cost of gasoline was extremely high throughout the world. That said, even in the best of times, some of the most expensive gas in the world is in Europe. To give the reader an idea of the cost of European gas, I took the average gasoline cost from eight major European countries including: the United Kingdom, France, Germany, Italy,

Greece, Belgium, Spain, and Norway. Adding all these countries together the average cost of a liter of gas is €2.103. The exchange rate for euros to dollars is 1.1. This calculation gave me a total cost, in dollars per liter of $2.313. Since you need 3.75 liters to make a gallon, you would multiply the dollars per liter times 3.75. (Cost per liter, $2.313 x   liters in a gallon, 3.75) This calculation gives you a total cost of gas in Europe of $8.67 per gallon. At this same point in time the average cost per gallon in the U.S. was $4.52. Still crazy high to Americans, but nothing compared to what you will pay in Europe. The numbers will change over time due to local prices and exchange rates, but generally expect gas in Europe to be roughly twice as expensive as what you would pay in the U.S. The chart below shows the total price, in dollars, for 1, 10, and 15 gallons of gas in Europe as of May 22nd, 2022.

2022 Gasoline Price per Gallon in Dollars		
Gallons	U.S.	Europe
1	$4.52	$8.67
10	$45.20	$86.70
15	$67.80	$130.05

    Ouch! Eye opening, isn't it? I chose the values in the gallons column as these are the most common gas tank sizes of cars that you might rent in Europe. The cars in Europe are generally smaller and thus have smaller gas tanks. You will not find many vehicles at rental companies in Europe that have larger than 15-gallon gas tanks. Just for comparison's sake, if we took the year when the exchange was the highest at $1.33, the cost per gallon would have been $10.46. Ten gallons (the tank size of normal small cars) would have cost you $104.60.

    To sum up renting cars in Europe, I would treat that as a last option as you compare costs and convenience as you plan your travel. If you can get by with only renting for a day here and there, then using taxis, buses and trains the other times, that would be best. Unfortunately, sometimes a car is needed to get where you want to go, just don't forget to calculate the total cost of renting a car.

Driving on the Wrong Side of the Road

Most of us think of the United Kingdom when we think about driving on the wrong side of the road. In fact, Ireland, Malta and Cyprus are three other European countries that drive on the left-hand side of the road. Driving on the left is a totally different beast as compared to driving in the U.S. In my opinion the most difficult thing about driving on the left is having to change the habits that you have established after driving for so many years on the right-hand side of the road. Driving on highways and larger streets is not so bad, but when you get into a big city where you may be driving on all types of roads and in stressful situations because you are not sure of exactly where you are going, it is considerably more difficult.

You will find yourself doing things just because "that is how you always do it" For example, when you arrive at an intersection, we naturally think that when I turn right, I need to stay in the right-hand lane. So, habit takes over and that is what you do. But wait, in this situation, you need to cross traffic and turn into the left-hand lane. A trick I use that helps me a little is to always think that the driver should be in the middle of the road, not on the outside. I also find that it helps to have someone sitting in the passenger seat to watch over what is happening. When habit takes over and you accidentally turn into the right-hand lane, they can let you know that you need to be in the other lane. Realize that driving on the "wrong" side of the road is just as nerve-racking for the passenger as it is for the driver. Just ask my wife.

Make sure that the car you rent has an automatic transmission. Many rentals in Europe will be manual transmissions. You have enough to worry about without considering shifting gears with your left hand rather than your right. I have driven anything from small cars to a 15-passenger van through London and the rest of the United Kingdom. It's tricky, it's a bit scary, and it is very stressful. I can tell you that the first place I went at the end of a day of driving in England, was the hotel bar. I don't want to scare anyone off. If you are a confident driver, you can certainly master driving on the wrong side of the road. Just don't underestimate the difficulty of the task.

Using the subway systems

Local subway systems are the best way to get around a European city. Most large cities will have a subway, or a streetcar system of some sort. This is because European citizens, due to their compact nature, rely much more heavily on public transportation than we do in America. The subway systems are easy to navigate, and the maps are equally easy to understand. The map below of the London Underground System is typical of what a subway map looks like.

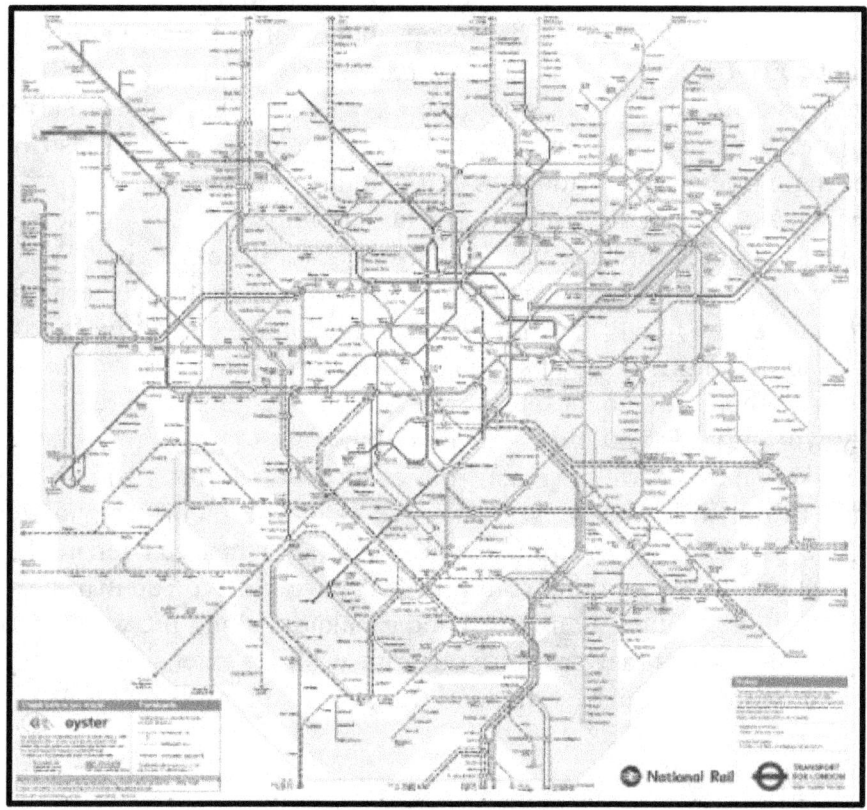

Figure 8: London Subway Map

The above map may look a little overwhelming, but it is actually very easy to read once you get a good look at it. Most city subway maps will look very similar to this one, with colored lines showing where trains go, where they stop, and when you need to switch trains to get to your destination. Most subway systems will also take you to transportation hubs such as airports or train stations that will take you outside the city if necessary. On the trains themselves, each car will have an easy-to-follow "line map" which will show you where you are, what the next stop is and which stops connect to other lines. If you have ridden the subway in a large U.S. city like Chicago or New York, the process is the same.

All subway systems will also have passes that you can purchase to make it easier to get around while you are staying in that city. The passes are usually for a specific time frame, such as a month, or a week. You might also get a pass for a given number of rides, such as a 10-ride ticket or a 15-ride ticket. Again, check out their websites if you want to get an idea in advance of what ticket options are available and which might suit your needs. There is no reason to buy these passes before you arrive in a country. They are easy to purchase at the subway stations, where vending machines that take credit cards will distribute the single ride or multi-ride pass that you desire to purchase.

In many cities, the subway and bus systems are part of the same system so tickets purchased at one may work for the other also. We will cover buses in the next section, just remember that each system is different, and you will need to research in advance or ask questions of locals to determine if the buses and subways work together.

One other point about the subway and rail systems is to realize that they will only get you close to where you want to go. You will more than likely need to walk to reach your exact destination. Also know that when riding the subway, you may have to walk some considerable distances to get from one train line to another, or when transferring from one station to another along your route. The walking you do in a subway station often includes many steps and escalators along the way. If you have health issues that prevent you from walking extensively, a rental car or taxi may be the best mode of transportation for you.

Using the bus systems

To be totally honest with you, I'm not a big fan of the bus systems, either in the U.S. or in Europe. It's not that they are inefficient, or any one thing is wrong with them, I'm just not a fan of riding the bus. I find bus systems much more difficult to navigate. It could be that I am just not smart enough to figure them out, but it seems much more difficult to map a route on a bus and then know for certain at which stop to get on and off to switch to another bus. In my opinion, it helps to know the city a little better in order to be good at using the bus system. With familiarity of the city, you know which direction certain streets go and the names and directions of the stops at the end of the route. The map below shows an image of the Paris bus system. You will find that bus maps are more difficult to read than the subway maps because by default the bus maps need to show all the streets in the map as well as the bus lines. In contrast, the subway maps really only need to show the lines and stops.

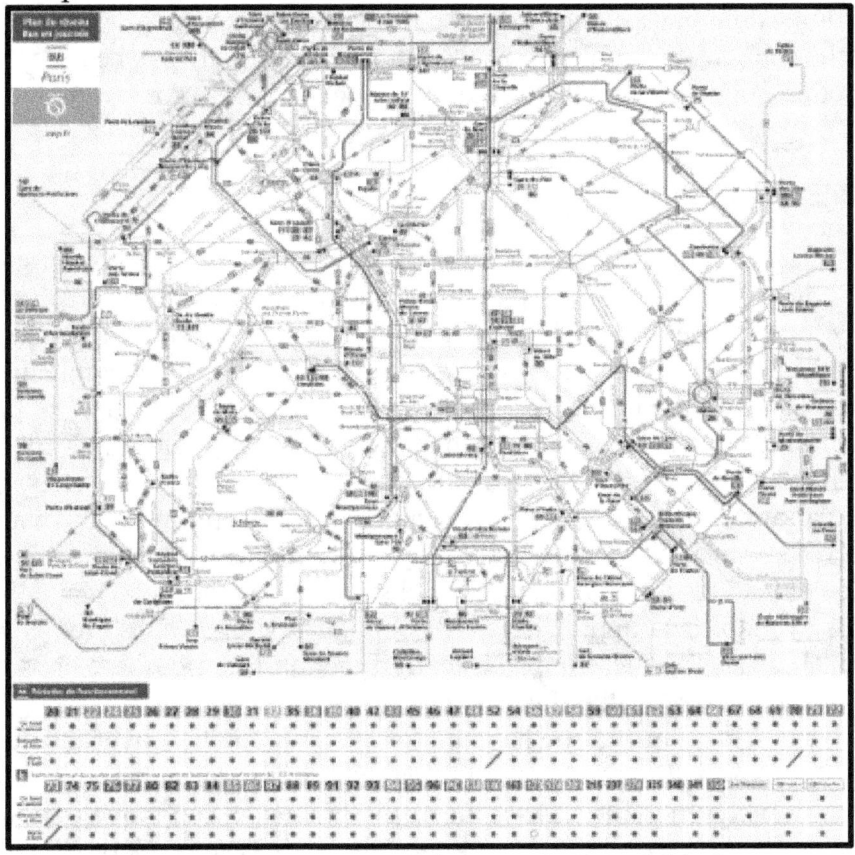

Figure 9: Paris Bus Map 2022 (courtesy of www.ratp.fr/en/)

That said, in some mid-size or smaller cities, buses may be your only choice. When I need to use the bus in Europe, I try to make sure that I ask either the station agent or the bus driver if I'm on the right bus. Sometimes the drivers are incredibly helpful, sometimes they are not. Usually there is someone on the bus who can tell you if you are on the right track as to where you are going. Tell the driver where you are trying to go and then sit near the front of the bus. If you are near the front the driver will often tell you when you need to get off. The good news is that most of the bus system websites have a trip planner tool that you can use to put in your starting point and final destination. The app will then tell you exactly which bus to get on and off and when to do so. You will often want to use the subway and bus systems in conjunction with each other to get you as close to your destination as possible.

Expect to need change to ride the bus. As mentioned in the subway section, some bus systems may use the same ticket system as that used by the subway, but some won't. Exact change will always be accepted. Another good reason to carry around a pocketful of euros.

Taxis and Ride Sharing

If getting directly to your destination quickly and without a great deal of walking is a priority for you, a taxi or rideshare service is the way to go. Of course, it is also likely the most expensive. The cost of these services is reduced if you are traveling with other companions who can share the cost of the ride with you. I'd love to be able to give you solid advice and practices that will apply to using taxis in any country in Europe. Unfortunately, taxi practices and rules and regulations differ not only by country, but also by city inside a country. Rideshare services such as Uber (www.uber.com) are available in most large cities in Europe. Some of these same large cities also make their taxis available via apps. The most popular taxi apps are "Free Now" and "Taxi EU". These apps basically function like rideshare apps but connect travelers with regular taxi cabs.

Taxi drivers in Europe have gotten a bad reputation over the years due to some bad apples taking advantage of travelers who are in a country where they are uncertain of the language, the money and the city. To be fair, the exact same things happen in New York or Chicago. Taxi drivers are no different than any other occupation. There are a few bad apples that give the other honest drivers a bad name. There are some basic things you can do to try and ensure that using a taxi is safe and to make it less likely for you to get cheated.

1. Ask for a price up front. The driver should at least be able to give you an estimate of the cost. Some cities have set prices to and from high traffic sites like airports or attractions.
2. At transportation hubs like airports and train stations, there will likely be a taxi queue where licensed and reputable cabs will line up and take the next person in line. Using this service, rather than just stepping into the street and "hailing" a cab, ensures you are getting a driver who has agreed to follow the rules. The person in charge of the queue may also be able to provide a price for the trip before you get in the cab.
3. Know the payment methods accepted before you get in the cab. Many taxis today will take credit cards, but some will not. If you plan to pay with a credit card, make sure you ask before getting into the cab if credit cards are an acceptable form of payment.
4. Have a basic idea of where you are going. Don't be afraid to ask the driver if it appears he is going in the wrong direction. He may know a better way, but you have at least informed him that you are watching to make sure he is going the right way. This is one of the beauties of the of the rideshare and taxi sharing apps in that you can follow on your phone where you are and where you are going. Even without an app, you should be able to follow your progress on your smartphone, assuming you have cell service.

Don't be afraid to use cabs. They are just another tool in your transportation arsenal that will help you get where you are going on your trip. If a site that you want to visit is a significant distance from the nearest bus or train station, a cab or rideshare service may be the best options to get you where you are going. Depending on your budget, it is sometimes better to pay the cost of a cab than walking over a mile to get somewhere. Yes, you will get there both ways, but you will be hot or cold and tired by the time you arrive if you choose to walk a significant distance. Don't forget that time spent walking is using valuable vacation time. You did not come to Europe to spend your time walking. That said, when traveling in Europe, wear comfortable shoes. You will be walking on a lot of uneven streets and cobblestones.

Don't be the Ugly American

To wrap up this guide on traveling in Europe I would be remiss if I didn't at least touch on how we, we as Americans, should act while in Europe, or really, anywhere outside the United States. Unfortunately, American travelers often have a less than positive reputation around the world. Some of this negativity is earned, while some of it likely comes from the fact that much of the television and movies that Europeans watch are from the U.S. and often do not present the most positive aspects of American society.

I'm going to list some individual things to consider below, but in general:

Don't be a Jerk!

How you act while abroad reflects on all Americans and if you behave badly, it reinforces the European image of the "ugly American". Don't be that guy. Always think of yourself as an ambassador for America and that your actions will influence the image that foreigners have of all of us. If something is not socially acceptable in the U.S., it is also not acceptable abroad. As a rule, try not to be noticed. This rule is not only good from a safety standpoint, but in regard to showing the rest of the world who we are and how we act.

The following list is a compilation from several different sources that show stereotypes of Americans across the world. Americans are:

- all rich
- don't do anything but party and have sex
- are loud, arrogant, and entitled
- don't know any language other than English
- don't know how to dress
- are committed to their jobs
- are overly patriotic
- are ignorant about the rest of the world

If we are honest, it's a little difficult to disagree with some of these stereotypes, but others are simply not true, or in the case of "overly patriotic" not necessarily a bad thing. Being loud, arrogant, and entitled is the one that promotes the image of the ugly American. This one should be easy for American travelers to avoid. Again, try not to be noticed. You are a guest in someone else's country, and you don't need to be the center of attention.

Here is a list of common-sense behaviors to consider when traveling in another country.

- Don't be loud. There is no reason to yell across a room, even if it is to your traveling party.
- Be polite and respectful to anyone you interact with: say please, thank you, you're welcome, excuse me etc., preferably in the local language.
- Be kind: open doors for others, wait your turn, follow local procedures
- Follow local rules: if something says, "Do not Touch". Don't touch it! Why would you think that is okay?

As Americans, let's all work together to improve our reputation around the world.

Conclusion

Of all the places in the world to visit, Europe is one of my favorites. It is one of the few places on earth that you can experience such a wide variety of culture, history, languages, and natural beauty in one easy to get to location. I'm a history buff, but others may go for the natural beauty, the amazing cuisine or just the variety of life experiences that can be seen in the many countries that make up the continent of Europe.

If I could give one piece of advice to anyone traveling outside of the U.S. it would be that cost is not everything. Obviously, it is much easier to travel in style with a larger budget. However, in my experience, some of the places that I have tried to save a few bucks have come back to haunt me as bad choices. In the end the cost saving was not worth the overall negative impact on my vacation experience. Always weigh the consequences of your choices in terms of stress as well as in regard to cost. For example, would you pay someone $10 to save an hour's worth of travel time? Is it worth $40 to get a room away from a busy street? Only you and your travel companions can make those decisions, but at least consider choices like this when making travel decisions

Hopefully this little guide has given you some tips for European travel no matter where you are in your planning for your trip. I have attempted to provide you with the options that are available to you as you travel. The reality is that one solution does not fit everyone's needs. A travelers' health, interests, budgets, and personal expectations all play a role in how you will choose to resolve issues that arise during your adventures. Have a great time in Europe.

If you enjoyed this book, please post an online review of the book on the platform of your choice. Online reviews are like currency to today's authors and any review you post would be most appreciated.

Post Review on the following platforms:

www.Amazon.com

www.Goodreads.com

www.BarnesandNoble.com

Go to www.jonathanjonesauthor to order signed copies of this and Jonathan's other books:

Moonlit Mayhem: Quantrill's Raid on Olathe, Kansas
Border War Tour
An American's Guide to European Travel

www.jonathanjonesauthor.com is also home to The Border War Tour history blog; a collection of blog posts about historical sites and events around the Kansas City area.

Appendix

Celsius to Fahrenheit Conversion Chart

Celsius to Fahrenheit	
Celsius	**Fahrenheit**
40	104
30	86
20	68
10	50
0	32
-10	14
-20	-4
-30	-22

10-year History of the Euro to Dollar Exchange Rate

10-year History of Euro to Dollar Conversion Rates	
Date	**1€ =**
December 31, 2013	$1.33
December 31, 2014	$1.33
December 31, 2015	$1.11
December 31, 2016	$1.11
December 31, 2017	$1.13
December 31, 2018	$1.18
December 31, 2019	$1.12
December 31, 2020	$1.14
December 31, 2021	$1.18
May 17, 2022	$1.10
Average	$13,173

An American's Guide to European Travel
Key Metric Conversions

Long Distance

Miles	Kilometers
1	1.60
10	16
50	80
100	160
200	320

Short Distance

Feet	Meters
1	0.30
10	3
50	15
100	30
200	60

Speed

Miles	Kilometers
40 mph	64 kph
60 mph	97 kph
80 mph	129 kph
100 mph	161 kph

Weight

Kilograms	Pounds
1	2.20
10	22.00
20	44
50	110
100	45

Liquid Volume

Gallons	Liters
1	3.75
10	38
15	57

Liquid Volume

Ounces	MiliLiters
6	177
11	330
16	473

An American's Guide to European Travel
Gasoline Price Chart

2022 Gasoline Price per Gallon in Dollars		
Gallons	U.S.	Europe
1	$4.52	$8.67
10	$45.20	$86.70
15	$67.80	$130.05

Bibliography

Abadi, Mark. "After traveling to 24 countries, I found people all around the world have the same 5 mistaken ideas about Americans." *BusinessInsider.com*, Insider, 23 June. 2018, www.businessinsider.com/american-stereotypes-travelers-hear-abroad-2018-1. Accessed 1 June 2022.

"EUR to USD Historical Exchange Rates." *OFX.com*, US Forex Inc, www.ofx.com/en-us/forex-news/historical-exchange-rates/eur/usd/. Accessed 18 May 2022.

"Plug & socket types around the world." *worldstandards.eu*, Worldstandards, www.worldstandards.eu/electricity/plugs-and-sockets/ . Accessed 1 June 2022.

Steves, Rick. "Tipping in Europe." *Rick Steve's Europe*, www.ricksteves.com/travel-tips/money/tipping-in-europe. Accessed 18 May 2022.

"The 6 Best Low-Cost Airlines in Europe." *Outofyourcomfortzone.net*, 3 Aug. 2021, www.outofyourcomfortzone.net/the-6-best-low-cost-airlines-in-europe/ . Accessed 1 June 2022.

"The top taxi apps by city: Europe edition." *travelperk.com*, TravelPerk S.L.U, www.travelperk.com/blog/top-taxi-apps-europe/ . Accessed 1 June 2022.

"Tourism in the EU - what a normal summer season looks like - before Covid-19." www.*ec.eruopa.eu*, ec.europa.eu/eurostat/statistics-explained/index.php?title=Tourism_in_the_EU_-_what_a_normal_summer_season_looks_like_-_before_Covid-19#:~:text=The%20main%20holiday%20season%20during,accommodation%20establishments%20across%20the%20EU. Accessed 1 June 2022.

About the Author

Jonathan Jones was born and raised in Harrisonville, Missouri. He graduated from Missouri State University with a BS in Business Education and from Park University, where he earned an MBA in International Business. Jones spent ten years as a teacher and coach in Missouri Schools before moving into the business world where he would spend the next 20+ years working as a business solutions specialist for IAT Insurance Group.

Jones is a lifelong history buff and spends much of his spare time researching history, both in his local area as well as traveling to visit historic sites around the world. Jones and his wife of 30 plus years, Jill, have three grown children, Zac, Lexi and Nikai and currently live in Olathe, Kansas. Jones has written three books, "Moonlit Mayhem: Quantrill's Raid of Olathe, Kansas", "Border War Tour" and "An American's Guide to European Travel." More information about Jones' work can be found by visiting www.JonathanJonesAuthor.com.

www.ingramcontent.com/pod-product-compliance
Lightning Source LLC
Chambersburg PA
CBHW072106110526
44590CB00018B/3340